AF301769

FSC
www.fsc.org
MIX
Papier aus ver-
antwortungsvollen
Quellen
Paper from
responsible sources
FSC® C105338

My World Lullaby

and other poems

Gabrielle von Bernstorff-Nahat

ISBN 9783757816483

Published and printed by:

BoD - Books on Demand,

Norderstedt, Germany

September 2023

This poem is dedicated to the memory of

Paolo Paolino

He was a young indigenous defender of the
Amazon Forest, who was unfortunately
murdered by illegal forest loggers.

His memory and embodied heroic actions live
on!

May all defenders for the wellbeing of this
beautiful planet and world be safe.

Preamble to My World Lullaby

The world is in great danger, she is in tragic
peril. The climate crisis is becoming more
intense with each day and season, species are
dying and imperialism and aggressive wars
trouble countries and millions of everyday
people, threatening their lives.

All the more reason to become active, to save the
planet, the climate, humanity and flora and
fauna. For this task we need to keep our spirits
high and our actions on the mark and well
tempered.

This lullaby intends to soothe and strengthen
your spirit. We must become like children again
and simply love and live our love for this

beautiful world, planet blue and you, in order to act well.

Find a quiet place, some solitude and meditate on the beauty of where we are. Don't forget the beauty and generous nature of the world in the middle of all its troubles. Strengthen your heart, body, soul and mind in order to be able to simply stand in awe, in love with this precious and fragile world.

This poem does not tell you what to do, but I hope it will strengthen your love for this beautiful planet and all its myriad of aspects and facets.

Become like a child again and reflect and contemplate the beauty and generosity of the world and then go out and make this world a brighter and better place within your sphere of influence, may it be large or small, the two belong together.

We sing lullabies to our children so that they may sleep and dream well. Please dream and act well!

My World Lullaby

This is my lullaby to the world

From me to you

My world song

She whispers to me

She whispers to you

She is fair, fragile, strong and beautiful

She is giving

So don't take too much

Don't take without returning

Stand by her and love her dearly

Her skies reach far and wide

From the sun to the moon

To the Milky Way stretching over the five
continents

And Africa is fair and good

And Europe is fair and good

And Asia is fair and good

And Australia is fair and good

And the Americas are fair and good

And all their people are fair and good

All people are born free, fair and good

And Italians are fair and good

And Kenyans are fair and good

And Egyptians are fair and good

And Ukranians are fair and good

And Indians are fair and good

And Iranians with their hair free are fair and
good

And Palestinians are fair and good

And Australians are fair and good

And Koreans are fair and good

And Israelis are fair and good

And Kurds are fair and good

And peace-loving Russians are fair and good

And Americans are fair and good

And South Africans are fair and good

And Afghans with their women free and
respected are fair and good

And Vietnamese are fair and good

And Taiwanese are fair and good

And Peruvians are fair and good

And Rhoynghas are fair and good

All countries are fine and good

And all their people are fair and good

All people are born free, fair and good

We are all fragile and warm

All our blood is the same red

All our flesh is made of this world

The same sun shines on all of us

We all have a soul

We partake in Soul together

We all love freedom

We come out of freedom and return to freedom

Freedom is our foundation

The universe's promise to us

We shall remain free

Free to love

Free to be with family loved ones and friends

Free to learn

Free to create

Free to shine

And the child is fair and good

And mothers are fair and good

And fathers are fair and good

And brothers, sisters, uncles and aunts, cousins
and nieces are all fair and good

And friends are fair and good

And foes are fair and good

All people are born fair and good

Our flesh is made of the same world

All our blood is the same red

We are all made of the same water

Whom does water belong to anyway?

Don't walk away

Rest with mankind, womankind and people

He, she, s-he, it they, them, us

We all are fine and fair and good

We are 10'000 years old and older

Endless

We are immortal souls

We have always been here and there and
everywhere

You've been a wanderer

And a king and a queen

And a merchant

And an artist

And a beggar

And a doctor

And a laborer

Who knows what this life is good for?

So be kind and understanding to every sentient
being

Hold each other

By your touch I am

By my touch you are

I am not without you

And you are not without me

United in our mutual differences

Loving in our different greatness

For we are all fine and fair and good

We are all born out of love

And we return to love

Planet blue is our home

Take tender care

And the skies are fair and good

And the clouds are fair and good

And the rains are fair and good

And snow is fair and good

And the seasons are fair and good

And spring is fair in good

And summer is fair and good

And fall is fair and good

And winter is fair and good

And the mountains are fine and great

And the valleys are fine and great

And the high seas are fine

And the low seas are fine

And dolphins and whales sing their songs

They are fair and fine

And the birds sing their songs

And they are fair and fine

We down here below soar with them

Without birds no sky

Without whales and dolphins no water

And the lion is fine and fair

And so is the gazelle

And so is every insect

Without them there would be no earth

We all inhabit this great space between sky and
earth

Take tender care

We breathe with the trees

We breathe with the roses

We breathe with the amazon

And Maples are fine and fair

All trees are fine and fair

And roses are fine and fair

All flowers are fine and fair

And the Amazon is fine and fair

All forests are fine and fair

And the Nile is fine and fair

All rivers are fine and fair

And the Himalaya is fine and fair

All mountains are fine and fair

We do not walk alone

The earth and the skies are the shoulders we
stand on

The new born babe lives between heaven and
earth

And so does its mother

And so does its father

And so does its sister

And so does its brother

And so do their offspring and their offspring

Their thoughts reach far and wide

So do their feelings and their dreams

The world is my song

My world lullaby

She whispers to me

And its monuments are fair and fine

And so are is the skyscraper, the house and the
straw hut

And its schools are fine

And its hospitals are fine

And its civic buildings are fine

And its cities are good and fair and fine

And Kiew is fine

And Khartoum will be fine again

And Bethlehem is fine

And Lausanne is fine

And Hanoi is fine

And Timbuktu is fine

And Perth is fine

And Johannesburg is fine

And Mexico City is fine

And Paris is fine

And Tokyo is fine

And Oslo is fine

And Christ Church is fine

And Istanbul is fine

And Lasa is fine

All cities are splendid and deserve brightness

And the piazza is fair and fine

And the mainstreet is fair and fine

And the town market is fair and fine

And the bazaar is fair and fine

This is where people meet and trade and where
children play

And that is fair and fine

Let the children play

Take care of all the children

Nourish the children and their parents

House children and their parents

Love all children and parents

Let the parents work and care for their children

And exchanging is fine

And trading is fine

And moving is fine

And climbing is fine

And thinking is fine

And weeping is fine

And dreaming is fine

And building is fine

And inventing is fine

What human beings do is fine and good

Human beings are fine and good

All people are born free, fine and good

And so is the beggar

And the one-legged woman

And the demonstrator

And the businesswoman

And the nurse

And the fireman

And the teacher

And the mentally ill

And the president

And the builder

And the doctor

And the artist

And the astronaut

All are fine and good and fair

All of us let the children play

Let all children learn

Give children love

Let all children live

Let all men, women, men and persons live

Love the homosexual

The lesbian

The transgender

The no-gender

Love all women, men, persons and children

Let all women, men and persons live

Give them water, food, shelter an occupation

Give them participatory politics

Give them a home, a village, a town and a city,
give them the country

Give them schools, hospitals and libraries

Give them fire-stations

Give them markets, shops, cafés, theatres and
music

Give them parks, pools and playgrounds

Give them peace and happiness

And the laborer does not ask much

And the cleaning woman does not ask much

And the farmer does not ask much

And the civil servant does not ask much

And the gardener does not ask much

Listen to the people

Child world

Woman world

Man world

Person world

God's garden is immeasurable

And peace is fine

And marriage is fine

And single is fine

And birth is fine

And dying returns us to the cycle of life and is
fine

And kissing is fine

And studying is fine

And making love is fine

And working is fine when it is fair

And playing is fine

We've been living like there is no tomorrow

But there will be

So, take tender care of planet blue and you and
them and us

This is my world song

She whispers to me, to you, to us

My world lullaby

My song to the world

Hear me fellow traveler

This is your voice

Hear me my friend

This is your voice

Hear me my lover

This is your voice

Hear me my companion

This is your voice

Hear me my foe

This is your voice too

You see me

I see you

We see each other

I love you

You love me

We love each other

We love the world

And she is fragile fair and good

The world is in your care

With its skies, sun, moon, stars and planets

With its seasons and the elements

With its soil, mountains and rivers, streams and
clouds

With its trees, its flora and fauna

With its birds, tigers, butterflies, bees and frogs

With its fish, crows, elephants and cows

With its generations, children, women, men and
people

With its houses, huts and towers

With its villages towns and cities

With its books, poetry, music and songs

With its crafts, pottery and gold

With its prayers, fragility and strength

With its love, intelligence and knowing

With its silence, sounds, sights and touches

Won't you be by her side

Her heart is beating

Listen to her

Feel her

Know her

Let her rock you to your soul

Make her a brighter place again

Make her a better place

Return her to her perfect self

Fall into her loving arms

Give her your devotion

Give back

Give her a future

Love her

Love her beauty

Go home to her

Smile at her

Plant the seeds of tomorrows bloom

Planet blue and you

And all that inhabit her

Listen to all cohabitants

Birds and bees

Elephants and mice

Himalayas and Mount Everests

Listen to every hill, grass and tree

Listen to its monuments, churches, temples and
mosques

Listen to her history and her stories and hear her
poetry

And then

Sing your world lullaby

And live your world song.

And other Poems

The doors which sometimes stay open

During the day

Open at night when we pass

Through desolation and pain

Your darkest moments will become

your brightest one day

Breaking through

Breaking through the walls of thinking hurts

Liquid shards in my mind

Covering the floor of my endless soul

The space between my wings is thick and great

Beyond memory there is seeing

You bring me bodies of light

We meet in the sun

My brain is blue

Black is beautiful

You know because you feel

My organs are made of gold

I feel your heartbeat

42 personal suns

You're wearing a red t-shirt

Universe endless heartbeat

May all children be well

Walls of light down here below

Above your heads

I can walk on the heads of mean

Light footed

Touch transforms

I am releasing more energy than a nuclear power
plant

Simultaneity is

Stop thinking

Beyond memory there is feeling

Another kind of knowing

Her dress is pure space

My better half takes me places

He knows my stars

Night Sky

Night sky over Bagdad

Star constellations have never been anywhere
but here

Down here on earth

Apples are blue

Rays of light

Liquid scattering my brain

Not in vain

Liquid milk of gold

Black milk

Heavy Milky Way

Speaking shards of fluid light

The sidewalk is my pillow case

Wandering with the dervishes

There is a cosmic record

Time

Heart of time

Without you I am not

I am with you

I've been waiting for you always

You my sun

Child, promise that you will love

Long ago she was carried by wings

Remembering

Persepolis

Far away impressions on the walls of her mind

He throws ink blotches

Into her forehead

Seat of the third eye

Beautiful rivers run

Murmering

Riders approach

I will be by your side

Her eyes see the invisible there is no distance

Everything is a vast inside

Like black ink shining

We touch each other

Perhaps this is all we ever do

Whom and what we have touched remains

All else fades

Milk and honey flowing through your veins

Treasure gently

Forget me not

Be strong

For there are hard times coming my love child

About the author

Gabrielle von Bernstorff-Nahat is a painter and writer. She exhibits her art work in Italy, Switzerland, Germany and in America. Her publications are all special edition art and poetry publications. Amongst her publications are titles such as: Touching, An Hommage to Malevich's Black Square, Color Writing, The Cosmos Within, You my Love and Poems of Tenderness, as well as the six volume series Nature Works consisting of the following titles: The Rock, Trees, Water, Air, For the Love of Dolphins and My Wandering Sun, Moon and Stars. Herr books are available at major online book shops, including amazon, fnac, orell füssli and bod.

Gabrielle currently lives in the beautiful Lake Constance region where she runs her open atelier and Tiny Gallery. More on her art work and books is to see on her website

www.gevebe.com